CONTENT CREATION: The New Gold Series 1

Table of Contents

SYNOPSIS

"Content Creation: The New Gold" is a captivating exploration of the evolving landscape of digital content and its immense value in the modern world. The synopsis of the book follows:

In **"Content Creation: The New Gold,"** renowned author and digital expert delves into the profound shift occurring in the global economy, where content creation has emerged as a precious resource, akin to gold. As traditional industries face disruption and technology continues to reshape our lives, the ability to create and distribute compelling content has become a lucrative and influential endeavor.

The book begins by tracing the historical significance of content creation, from ancient storytelling to the advent of the printing press and the subsequent democratization of information. It highlights how the internet and social media revolutionized content consumption, empowering individuals and businesses alike to produce and disseminate their creations to a vast audience.

Drawing on a rich tapestry of case studies, real-life examples, and interviews with content creators across various mediums, the author explores the multifaceted nature of content creation. From viral YouTube videos and podcasting sensations to influential bloggers and Instagram influencers, the book examines the diverse forms of content that capture the attention and engagement of millions.

Through insightful analysis, the author unveils the underlying principles and strategies that make content creation successful. From understanding target audiences and leveraging storytelling techniques to harnessing the power of data analytics and emerging technologies, the book provides invaluable guidance for aspiring content creators and established professionals seeking to enhance their craft.

Moreover, **"Content Creation: The New Gold"** delves into the economic implications of this burgeoning industry. It explores the monetization models employed by content creators, such as brand partnerships, sponsorships, crowdfunding, and digital subscriptions. The book also addresses the ethical considerations and challenges surrounding content creation, including issues of authenticity, transparency, and the impact of algorithmic platforms on content discovery and distribution.

As the book concludes, it underscores the immense opportunities that lie ahead in the realm of content creation. With the increasing demand for quality, personalized content, individuals and businesses can tap into this new economy, capitalizing on their unique voices, talents, and expertise.

"Content Creation: The New Gold" serves as an inspiring and informative guide for anyone seeking to understand and thrive in the dynamic world of digital content. It illuminates the transformative power of creativity, innovation, and strategic thinking, demonstrating how content creation has become the contemporary currency for success.

INTRODUCTION

In today's interconnected and digitized world, content creation has emerged as a powerful force, shaping the way we consume information, engage with others, and make decisions. The ability to create compelling and engaging content has become not just an art form but also a valuable commodity—a new form of gold that holds immense potential and opportunities.

"**Content Creation: The New Gold**" is a thought-provoking exploration of this rapidly evolving landscape. In this book, we embark on a journey to understand the profound impact content creation has had on society, businesses, and individuals. We delve into the historical roots of storytelling, tracing its transformation through the ages, and examine how technological advancements have revolutionized the way content is created, distributed, and consumed.

The internet and social media platforms have become the modern-day marketplace for content, offering a level playing field for creators to share their ideas, perspectives, and talents with a global audience. Whether it's a viral video on YouTube, a thought-provoking blog post, or a captivating podcast, the power of content to captivate, inspire, and influence is undeniable.

In this book, we explore the diverse forms of content creation that have risen to prominence, examining the strategies and principles that underpin their success. From understanding the needs and desires of target audiences to leveraging the art of storytelling and harnessing the capabilities of data analytics and emerging technologies, we uncover the secrets behind creating content that resonates.

Furthermore, **"Content Creation: The New Gold"** addresses the economic dimensions of this industry. We delve into the various monetization models employed by content creators, exploring how they turn their creative endeavors into viable businesses. From brand partnerships and sponsorships to crowdfunding and digital subscriptions, we explore the evolving ways in which content creators can monetize their work while maintaining authenticity and integrity.

However, as content creation takes center stage, ethical considerations and challenges also come into play. We examine the ethical dilemmas surrounding content creation, including issues of transparency, authenticity, and the impact of algorithmic platforms on content discovery and distribution. As content creators navigate this evolving landscape, it becomes essential to strike a balance between commercial success and maintaining trust with their audiences.

In **"Content Creation: The New Gold,"** we not only analyze the present state of content creation but also glimpse into its future. We discuss the emerging trends and technologies that will shape the industry, offering insights into the opportunities and challenges that lie ahead. With the democratization of content creation, the power to influence and make a difference has never been more accessible.

This book aims to inspire aspiring content creators and provide valuable guidance to established professionals seeking to refine their craft. It is a testament to the transformative power of creativity, innovation, and strategic thinking, reminding us that in this digital age, content creation has become the currency for success.

Join us as we embark on this exciting journey into the world of **"Content Creation: The New Gold."** Let us explore together the immense possibilities and the boundless potential that lie within this dynamic industry.

CHAPTER 1

THE RISE OF CONTENT CREATION

The digital age has witnessed a significant rise in the importance of content creation. With the proliferation of the internet, social media platforms, and digital technologies, the demand for high-quality content has never been greater. Content creation encompasses various forms, including articles, blog posts, videos, podcasts, infographics, and social media posts. In this era, individuals, businesses, and organizations are recognizing the immense value of content creation as a means of communication, engagement, and brand building.

One of the key reasons for the growing importance of content creation is the shift in consumer behavior. Traditional marketing techniques are becoming less effective, as consumers are increasingly seeking authentic, valuable, and personalized content. They are actively searching for information, entertainment, and solutions to their problems. By creating compelling and relevant content, businesses and individuals can establish themselves as trusted authorities in their respective fields and engage with their target audience effectively.

Content creation also plays a crucial role in enhancing brand visibility and online presence. With the rise of social media platforms and search engines, content is the currency that drives engagement and drives traffic. High-quality content that is optimized for search engines can improve a website's search rankings, making it more discoverable to potential customers. Moreover, engaging and shareable content on social media platforms can significantly expand the reach of a brand, allowing it to connect with a broader audience.

Furthermore, content creation fosters deeper connections and relationships with the audience. By providing valuable and insightful content, businesses can establish a sense of trust and credibility with their customers. Content that educates, entertains, or solves a problem can resonate with the audience on an emotional level, creating a lasting impression and driving customer loyalty.

In addition to its impact on brand building and audience engagement, content creation also serves as a catalyst for thought leadership and industry influence. By consistently producing high-quality content, individuals and organizations can position themselves as experts in their respective domains. This can lead to various opportunities such as speaking engagements, collaborations, partnerships, and media exposure, further enhancing their reputation and influence.

The accessibility of content creation tools and platforms has also contributed to its rise. The barrier to entry for creating and sharing content has significantly decreased, allowing individuals and businesses of all sizes to participate. Social media platforms, blogging platforms, video-sharing platforms, and podcasting platforms provide accessible and user-friendly interfaces for content creation and distribution.

However, it is important to note that with the rise of content creation, there is also an increase in the volume of content available. This saturation poses a challenge for content creators to stand out from the crowd and produce content that truly resonates with their target audience. Quality, relevance, and authenticity are key factors that determine the success of content creation efforts.

In conclusion, the growing importance of content creation in the digital age is driven by changing consumer behavior, the need for brand visibility and engagement, the desire for authentic connections, and the democratization of content creation tools. By creating valuable and relevant content, individuals and businesses can establish their presence, build relationships, and influence their industries. As the digital landscape continues to evolve, content creation will remain a vital component of successful online strategies.

CHAPTER 2

CONTENT CREATION AS A CAREER

In the digital age, content creation has emerged as a viable and lucrative career path for individuals who are passionate about creating and sharing valuable content. Here are some ways in which individuals are turning their passion for content creation into a profession:

1. Freelancing: Many content creators choose to work as freelancers, offering their services to businesses, agencies, and individuals. They create content such as blog posts, articles, social media posts, videos, or podcasts on a project basis. Freelancers can build a portfolio of their work, establish relationships with clients, and charge competitive rates based on their expertise and experience.

2. Blogging/Vlogging: Blogging and vlogging have become popular avenues for content creators to share their expertise and interests. By creating a blog or YouTube channel and consistently producing high-quality content, individuals can attract an audience and monetize their platforms through advertising, sponsored content, brand partnerships, and affiliate marketing. Successful bloggers and vloggers often diversify their income streams by creating digital products, offering online courses, or organizing events.

3. Social Media Influencing: Content creators with a strong social media presence can collaborate with brands and businesses to promote products or services. Influencers leverage their engaged audience to create sponsored content, brand endorsements, and collaborations. They can monetize their platforms through sponsored posts, affiliate marketing, sponsored events, and partnerships. Building an authentic and engaged community is key to success as a social media influencer.

4. Content Writing: Content writers specialize in creating written content for various platforms, including websites, blogs, magazines, and digital publications. They may work as full-time employees or freelancers for businesses, marketing agencies, or media outlets. Content writers need strong writing skills, the ability to research and adapt to different topics, and a good understanding of SEO (Search Engine Optimization) techniques to optimize their content for search engines.

5. Video Production: With the rise of video platforms like YouTube and the popularity of video content, individuals skilled in video production can turn their passion into a career. They can create and produce videos for various purposes, including educational content, entertainment, marketing campaigns, and documentaries. Video creators can monetize their content through advertising, brand partnerships, and sponsored videos.

6. Podcasting: Podcasting has gained significant popularity, providing an avenue for individuals to share their expertise and interests through audio content. Content creators can host their own podcasts, interview guests, discuss topics of interest, and provide valuable insights to their audience. Podcasters can generate revenue through sponsorships, advertisements, and listener donations.

To succeed as a content creator, individuals should focus on developing their skills, building their personal brand, and consistently producing high-quality content that resonates with their target audience. Building a strong online presence, networking with other creators, and staying updated with industry trends are also crucial for long-term success in this field.

CHAPTER 3

MONETIZING CONTENT

Content creators have several strategies and platforms available to monetize their work and generate income.

Here are some popular methods:

1. Advertising: Content creators can earn revenue through advertising by displaying ads on their websites, blogs, YouTube videos, or podcasts. They can join ad networks like Google AdSense, which match relevant ads to their content, or work directly with brands for sponsored ads. The revenue generated depends on factors such as the number of views, clicks, or impressions.

2. Sponsorships and Brand Partnerships: Collaborating with brands and businesses can be a lucrative way to monetize content. Content creators can partner with brands that align with their niche and create sponsored content, product reviews, or endorsements. They may receive payment, free products, or affiliate commissions for promoting the brand to their audience.

3. Affiliate Marketing: Content creators can join affiliate programs and earn a commission for driving sales or leads through their content. They can include affiliate links in blog posts, video descriptions, or social media posts to recommend products or services. Platforms like Amazon Associates, ShareASale, or Commission Junction offer a wide range of affiliate programs.

4. Digital Products: Creating and selling digital products can be a profitable monetization strategy. Content creators can develop e-books, online courses, tutorials, templates, or stock resources related to their niche. They can sell these products on their websites, through platforms like Gumroad or Teachable, or use e-commerce platforms like Shopify.

5. Crowdfunding and Donations: Platforms like Patreon, Ko-fi, or Buy Me a Coffee allow content creators to receive recurring or one-time payments from their audience as a form of support or appreciation. Creators can offer exclusive content, early access, or special perks to their supporters in return.

6. Sponsored Content and Guest Posts: Content creators can offer sponsored content opportunities on their platforms, where businesses or individuals pay to have their content featured. Additionally, they can monetize their authority and expertise by accepting paid guest posts from other writers or businesses in their niche.

7. Events, Workshops, and Speaking Engagements: Content creators can leverage their expertise and audience to host events, workshops, or speaking engagements. They can charge admission fees or secure sponsorship for these activities, providing valuable in-person or online experiences to their audience.

8. Licensing and Syndication: Content creators can license their content, such as articles, photos, or videos, to other platforms, publications, or businesses for a fee. Syndication allows creators to distribute their content to multiple platforms simultaneously, reaching a wider audience and generating income through licensing agreements.

It's important for content creators to choose monetization strategies that align with their audience, niche, and personal goals. Diversifying income streams can provide stability and flexibility. Content creators should also consider factors like audience engagement, niche demand, and evolving trends to adapt their monetization strategies over time.

CHAPTER 4

THE POWER OF VISUAL CONTENT

Visual content, including videos and images, holds immense power in engaging audiences and building online communities. Humans are inherently visual beings, and visual content appeals to our senses, emotions, and cognitive processes. Here are some ways visual content creates an impact:

1. Grabbing Attention: Visual content has a remarkable ability to capture attention quickly. With the increasing volume of online content, visuals help content creators stand out amidst the noise. Compelling images or striking video thumbnails can grab the viewer's attention, prompting them to explore further.

2. Enhancing Communication: Visual content often communicates messages more effectively than text alone. Images and videos can convey complex ideas, emotions, or concepts in a concise and visually appealing manner. They help break down barriers of language, culture, and literacy, enabling a wider audience to understand and connect with the content.

3. Evoking Emotions: Visual content has a potent emotional impact. The power of images and videos lies in their ability to evoke a range of emotions, from joy and inspiration to sadness and empathy. Emotionally resonant visual content can leave a lasting impression on viewers and create a deep sense of connection with the creator and the community.

4. Increasing Engagement: Visual content is highly engaging, leading to increased viewer interactions and participation. Videos, in particular, can hold attention for longer periods compared to other content formats. Engaging visuals, such as eye-catching graphics or well-edited videos, encourage viewers to like, comment, share, and subscribe, fostering a sense of community and participation.

5. Building Brand Identity: Visual content plays a vital role in establishing and reinforcing a brand's identity. Consistent visual elements, such as logos, color schemes, and visual styles, create a recognizable and memorable brand image. Visual content helps shape brand perception and establishes a cohesive identity that resonates with the target audience.

6. Facilitating Storytelling: Visual content is a powerful tool for storytelling. Through images and videos, content creators can convey narratives, share experiences, and evoke emotions in a way that engages and captivates the audience. Visual storytelling builds a connection between the creator and the community, fostering a sense of authenticity and trust.

7. Encouraging Sharing and Virality: Visual content is highly shareable, leading to its potential for virality. Compelling and visually appealing content is more likely to be shared across social media platforms, expanding its reach and attracting new viewers and community members. This sharing culture helps content creators grow their audience and build online communities.

8. Providing Educational Value: Visual content is effective in delivering educational information. Videos, tutorials, infographics, and diagrams can simplify complex topics, making them easier to understand and retain. Visual content enhances the learning experience and encourages knowledge sharing within online communities.

In conclusion, visual content holds significant power in engaging audiences and building online communities. Its ability to captivate attention, evoke emotions, enhance communication, and facilitate storytelling creates a profound impact on content creators and their audiences. By leveraging the power of visual content, creators can forge strong connections, foster community engagement, and establish a memorable brand presence in the digital landscape.

CHAPTER 5

CONTENT CREATION FOR SOCIAL MEDIA

Creating compelling content for social media platforms requires thoughtful planning and execution. Here are some tips and techniques to help you create engaging content for popular social media platforms like Instagram, YouTube, TikTok, and more:

1. Understand Your Target Audience: Gain a deep understanding of your target audience's preferences, interests, and demographics. This knowledge will help you create content that resonates with them and captures their attention.

2. Consistent Branding: Establish a consistent visual style, tone of voice, and overall branding across your social media platforms. Consistency helps build recognition and reinforces your brand identity.

3. Use Eye-Catching Visuals: Visuals play a crucial role in capturing attention on social media. Use high-quality images, videos, graphics, and animations that are visually appealing, engaging, and shareable. Experiment with different formats, filters, and effects to stand out.

4. Embrace Storytelling: Tell compelling stories through your content. Storytelling creates an emotional connection with your audience, making your content more memorable and shareable. Incorporate narratives, personal experiences, and relatable situations into your posts or videos.

5. Incorporate User-Generated Content: Encourage your audience to create and share content related to your brand or niche. User-generated content not only adds authenticity but also fosters a sense of community and engagement. Repost and give credit to users who create content relevant to your brand.

6. Optimize Captions and Descriptions: Craft engaging captions and descriptions that complement your visual content. Use relevant hashtags, emojis, and call-to-actions to encourage interaction and discoverability. Consider using storytelling, humor, or asking questions to stimulate engagement.

7. Utilize Influencer Collaborations: Collaborating with influencers relevant to your niche can help expand your reach and tap into their existing audience. Seek influencers whose values align with your brand, and consider co-creating content or running contests or giveaways together.

8. Leverage Platform-Specific Features: Each social media platform offers unique features and formats. Tailor your content to leverage these features effectively. For instance, Instagram Stories, IGTV, or Reels; YouTube live streaming or premieres; TikTok's short-form videos and trends. Stay updated with platform updates and trends to stay relevant.

9. Engage with Your Audience: Social media is all about community and conversation. Respond to comments, messages, and mentions from your audience. Encourage discussions, ask for opinions, and actively engage with your followers. This fosters a sense of connection and loyalty.

10. Analyze and Iterate: Regularly analyze your content performance using platform insights and analytics tools. Identify what works well, understand audience engagement patterns, and adapt your content strategy accordingly. Experiment with different content types, posting times, and themes to refine your approach.

Remember, creating compelling content for social media requires a combination of creativity, authenticity, and adaptability. Stay true to your brand's voice and values while keeping your audience's preferences in mind. Keep experimenting, learning from your audience's feedback, and evolving your content strategy to stay ahead in the ever-changing social media landscape.

CHAPTER 6

BUILDING A PERSONAL BRAND THROUGH CONTENT

Content creation plays a pivotal role in building a personal brand and opening up professional opportunities for individuals. Here's how content creation can help establish a personal brand and enhance professional growth:

1. Showcasing Expertise: By creating and sharing valuable content within their area of expertise, individuals can position themselves as knowledgeable and credible authorities in their field. Consistently producing high-quality content demonstrates expertise, attracts a relevant audience, and establishes trust with followers and potential clients or employers.

2. Differentiating from Competitors: Content creation allows individuals to showcase their unique perspectives, skills, and personality. It helps them stand out from competitors by offering a distinctive voice and point of view. Building a personal brand through content helps individuals carve a niche and be recognized for their expertise and unique approach.

3. Growing an Engaged Audience: Content creation serves as a means to connect with an audience and build a community around one's personal brand. By consistently sharing valuable content, individuals can attract and engage like-minded individuals, fostering relationships and collaborations. An engaged audience can lead to increased professional opportunities such as speaking engagements, partnerships, or consulting opportunities.

4. Building Trust and Credibility: Creating content that is informative, helpful, and relevant helps build trust and credibility with the audience. Sharing insights, advice, or thought leadership content demonstrates expertise and establishes individuals as trusted resources in their field. As trust grows, it becomes easier to attract clients, customers, or employers who value their expertise.

5. Networking and Collaborations: Content creation opens doors for networking and collaboration opportunities. Engaging with others in the industry, featuring guest contributors, or participating in collaborations with other content creators helps expand reach, tap into new audiences, and build professional relationships. Collaborations can lead to cross-promotion, joint ventures, and increased exposure.

6. Enhancing Online Presence: Content creation strengthens an individual's online presence, making them discoverable to potential clients, employers, or collaborators. Well-optimized content can improve search engine rankings, increasing visibility and attracting opportunities. A strong online presence also helps individuals control their personal narrative and shape public perception.

7. Professional Development and Learning: Content creation requires research, staying up-to-date with industry trends, and continuously honing skills. This process of creating content helps individuals stay informed and knowledgeable in their field. The journey of content creation also presents opportunities for personal and professional growth, as individuals gain new insights, learn from their audience, and refine their expertise.

8. Leveraging Multiple Platforms: Content creation allows individuals to leverage various platforms and mediums to reach a broader audience. Whether it's blogging, podcasting, creating videos, or social media content, each platform offers unique opportunities to engage with different audiences and expand professional reach.

In conclusion, content creation serves as a powerful tool for individuals to establish a personal brand, demonstrate expertise, and unlock professional opportunities. Through consistent and valuable content creation, individuals can differentiate themselves, grow their audience, and build trust and credibility. By leveraging their personal brand, individuals can attract clients, customers, partnerships, speaking engagements, and various other professional opportunities.

CHAPTER 7

STORYTELLING IN CONTENT CREATION

Storytelling is a powerful and fundamental aspect of content creation that can make your content captivating, memorable, and emotionally engaging. Here's a closer look at the art of storytelling and its significance in content creation:

1. Capturing Attention: Stories have the ability to capture attention from the very beginning. By starting your content with an engaging narrative or a compelling hook, you can immediately draw in your audience and pique their curiosity, making them more likely to continue consuming your content.

2. Creating Emotional Connection: Stories tap into emotions and create a deeper connection with the audience. By incorporating relatable characters, evoking emotions, and building narratives around human experiences, you can elicit empathy, inspire, entertain, or even challenge your audience's perspectives. Emotional engagement leads to a more memorable and impactful content experience.

3. Making Complex Ideas Accessible: Storytelling allows you to simplify and communicate complex ideas or concepts effectively. By presenting information in a narrative format, you can break down intricate topics into relatable and understandable stories. This helps your audience grasp and retain the information more easily.

4. Building Memorable Content: Stories are memorable. When you weave narratives into your content, it becomes more memorable and sticks in the minds of your audience. By creating memorable content, you increase the chances of your audience recalling and sharing it with others, thus extending the reach of your message.

5. Fostering Engagement and Connection: Storytelling encourages engagement and fosters a sense of connection with your audience. By crafting narratives that resonate with their experiences, aspirations, or challenges, you create a shared understanding and build a stronger bond. Engaged audiences are more likely to interact, comment, and share your content, enhancing its reach and impact.

6. Conveying Values and Purpose: Stories offer a powerful way to communicate your values, mission, or purpose as a content creator. By incorporating narratives that align with your core beliefs, you can connect with an audience that shares those values. This helps build a community of like-minded individuals who are passionate about your content and more likely to support your brand.

7. Promoting Authenticity and Relatability: Authenticity is crucial in content creation, and storytelling allows you to showcase your authentic self. By sharing personal experiences, lessons learned, or challenges faced, you create a relatable and genuine connection with your audience. This builds trust and loyalty, making your content more influential and impactful.

8. Encouraging Action and Impact: Stories have the power to inspire action. By crafting narratives that convey a call-to-action or a purpose-driven message, you can motivate your audience to take specific steps, whether it's making a change, supporting a cause, or adopting new behaviors. Stories that inspire action have a lasting impact on individuals and communities.

Incorporating storytelling techniques in your content creation involves understanding your audience, developing engaging narratives, and delivering your message in a compelling way. By leveraging the art of storytelling, you can create content that resonates, captivates, and leaves a lasting impression on your audience.

CHAPTER 8

CONTENT CREATION FOR SEO

Content creation plays a crucial role in search engine optimization (SEO). Search engines like Google prioritize high-quality, relevant, and valuable content when ranking web pages. By creating SEO-friendly content, you can increase your visibility in search engine results pages (SERPs) and attract organic traffic to your website. Here's an overview of the role of content creation in SEO and some best practices to follow:

1. Relevance and Keyword Research:

- Understand your target audience and their search intent.

- Conduct keyword research to identify relevant keywords and phrases.

- Incorporate target keywords naturally into your content.

2. Quality and Value:

- Create original, well-written content that provides value to your audience.

- Focus on solving problems, answering questions, or addressing needs.

- Offer unique insights, in-depth analysis, or practical tips to stand out.

3. User Experience and Readability:

- Structure your content with headings, subheadings, and bullet points.

- Use clear and concise language to make your content easy to understand.

- Break up long paragraphs and use shorter sentences for better readability.

4. On-Page Optimization:

- Optimize your title tag, meta description, and URL for relevant keywords.

- Use descriptive and compelling titles to entice clicks in the SERPs.

- Include relevant keywords in headings, but prioritize user readability.

5. Formatting and Multimedia:

- Use proper formatting with tags (e.g., <h1>, <h2>, <p>) for better HTML structure.

- Incorporate relevant images, videos, infographics, or other multimedia.

- Optimize multimedia elements with alt tags and descriptive file names.

6. Link Building:

- Create content that naturally attracts backlinks from reputable websites.

- Include internal links to other relevant pages on your website.

- Reach out to other webmasters or influencers for potential link opportunities.

7. Mobile-Friendliness and Page Speed:

- Ensure your content is mobile-responsive and displays well on all devices.

- Optimize your website's loading speed to improve user experience.

- Compress images, leverage caching, and minimize unnecessary scripts.

8. Regular Updates and Fresh Content:

- Keep your content up to date, especially for time-sensitive topics.

- Add new content regularly to demonstrate ongoing relevance.

- Consider repurposing or updating existing content to extend its lifespan.

9. Social Media Promotion:

- Share your content on social media platforms to increase visibility.

- Encourage social sharing and engagement to expand your reach.

- Engage with your audience and respond to comments and inquiries.

Remember, SEO is a long-term strategy, and it takes time to see results. By consistently creating high-quality, SEO-friendly content, you can improve your website's visibility, attract organic traffic, and enhance your overall online presence.

CONCLUSION

"Content Creation: The New Gold" has taken us on a captivating exploration of the ever-evolving landscape of content creation and its profound impact on our world. We have witnessed how content creation has become the contemporary currency for success, offering individuals and businesses a platform to share their stories, insights, and talents with a global audience.

Throughout this book, we have discovered the historical significance of storytelling and the transformative power of technology, which has democratized the creation and distribution of content. From viral YouTube videos to influential bloggers and Instagram influencers, we have seen the diverse forms of content that captivate and engage millions.

We have delved into the principles and strategies that underpin successful content creation, exploring the art of understanding target audiences, crafting compelling narratives, and harnessing data analytics and emerging technologies. By mastering these skills, content creators can stand out in a crowded digital landscape and create content that resonates with their audiences.

Moreover, we have explored the economic implications of content creation, examining the various monetization models that enable content creators to turn their passion into a viable business. From brand partnerships to crowdfunding and digital subscriptions, we have witnessed the creative ways in which creators can monetize their content while maintaining their authenticity and ethical integrity.

However, we have also acknowledged the ethical considerations and challenges that come with content creation. Transparency, authenticity, and the impact of algorithmic platforms are crucial factors that content creators must navigate carefully to build and maintain trust with their audiences.

As we conclude our journey, we recognize that content creation is an ever-evolving field. The future holds exciting possibilities as emerging technologies, such as virtual reality, augmented reality, and artificial intelligence, continue to shape the way we consume and create content. By staying adaptable and embracing innovation, content creators can seize new opportunities and stay ahead in this dynamic industry.

"Content Creation: The New Gold" serves as a guide for aspiring content creators and a source of inspiration for established professionals seeking to refine their craft. It reminds us that in an interconnected world driven by digital content, creativity, innovation, and strategic thinking are the keys to success.

As content creators, let us embrace our roles as storytellers, thought leaders, and influencers. Let us leverage the power of content creation to inspire, educate, entertain, and make a positive impact on the world. In this new era, content creation truly shines as the new gold, enriching lives, fostering connections, and unlocking limitless possibilities.

EPILOGUE

In this epilogue, we reflect on the transformative journey we have taken in exploring the world of **"Content Creation: The New Gold."** We have witnessed the immense value and influence of content creation, the evolving landscape it inhabits, and the opportunities it presents.

Since the publication of this book, the realm of content creation has continued to evolve at a rapid pace. Emerging technologies have further disrupted traditional forms of content, giving rise to new mediums and platforms that continue to shape the way we create, consume, and interact with content.

Virtual reality and augmented reality have become increasingly prevalent, offering immersive and interactive experiences that push the boundaries of storytelling. Artificial intelligence and machine learning algorithms are enabling personalized content recommendations, making it easier for audiences to discover content that aligns with their interests and preferences.

Furthermore, the democratization of content creation has reached new heights, with social media platforms and online communities becoming breeding grounds for new voices, ideas, and movements. Individuals from diverse backgrounds can now make their mark in the content landscape, challenging traditional gatekeepers and amplifying marginalized perspectives.

However, as the industry expands, new challenges and considerations have emerged. Issues surrounding digital rights, intellectual property, and privacy have become increasingly important for content creators and consumers alike. Navigating these complexities while maintaining ethical standards and fostering meaningful connections with audiences has become a critical aspect of successful content creation.

In the years since the publication of **"Content Creation: The New Gold,"** countless success stories have emerged, showcasing the power of content to transform lives and businesses. From independent creators who have built thriving communities around their content to organizations that have leveraged content as a means of building brand loyalty and customer engagement, the impact of content creation continues to grow.

As we look to the future, we can envision a world where content creation becomes even more intertwined with our daily lives. The lines between creator and consumer may continue to blur as technology enables greater interactivity and collaboration, giving rise to co-creation and user-generated content that reflects the collective voice of communities.

In this ever-evolving landscape, it is crucial for content creators to stay adaptable, innovative, and mindful of the ethical implications of their work. The journey of content creation is one of continuous learning, experimentation, and growth. It requires a deep understanding of audiences, a commitment to storytelling, and an unwavering dedication to authenticity and integrity.

"Content Creation: The New Gold" serves as a timeless reminder of the value and potential that lies within content creation. It reminds us that in this digital age, content creation is not just a means of communication but a catalyst for change, empowerment, and connection.

As we move forward, let us embrace the power of content creation to shape narratives, inspire others, and make a positive impact. Let us recognize the opportunities that lie within our reach and harness our creative abilities to turn ideas into reality. Together, we can continue to mine the new gold of content creation, forging a future where creativity and innovation know no bounds.